The Republic Of Love

Twenty-five Poems
by
MICHAEL MURPHY

LIB
ERT
IES

'A significant number of couples have already availed of the civil partnership registration process. . . . For some, it is an opportunity to recognise their lifelong love in public, to give visibility to the normality of homosexual identity, and to speak eloquently about Ireland moving towards *"the republic of love"*. The latter phrase, which comes from a poem by Michael Murphy for his partner, Terry O'Sullivan, was one of the most recent attempts to put into language the achievements of the legislation.'

Senator Dr Katherine Zappone, speaking in Seanad Éireann, the Upper House of the Irish Parliament, on Wednesday, 13 July 2011

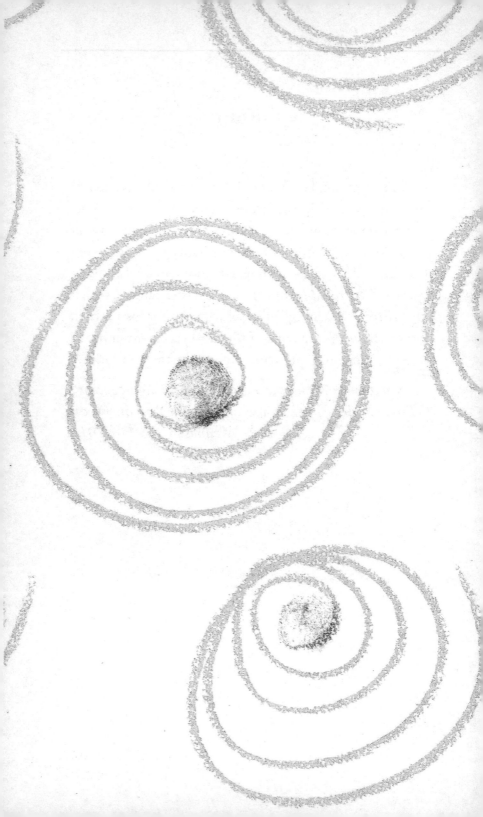

Contents

Foreword
Dr Jeannine Woods

*'Wear the clothes of the love story
of your life . . .'*

Michael Murphy's life and work have long demon-
strated an engagement with language. His beautiful
voice is familiar and beloved by many in his role as a
newscaster and broadcaster on Ireland's national radio
and television station, RTÉ. Michael's private work as a
psychoanalyst, recently seen publicly in his weekly
thoughtful contributions to the afternoon *Today Show*
on television, draws on a deep understanding of the role
of language in unearthing and articulating penumbral
facets of life and experience. In its courage and lucidity,
the publication of Michael's searingly honest memoir, *At
Five in the Afternoon – My Battle with Male Cancer*, in
2009 introduced its readers to a deeply personal register
of Michael's voice, the voice of the writer, and includes
some of the poems which form part of this collection,
appearing here devoid of context, exposing a naked
voice, open, honest, trusting.

The poems in this volume are organised under different headings centred around various themes and motifs, weaving together the threads of language, sensuousness and emotional experience. The cadence and musicality of the *Flowers* poems affirm and celebrate the presence of life in the face of change and loss, while the poems under the heading of *Emotion* reflect a fearless engagement with the inner and outer worlds, in their insistence on confronting the 'dignified silence' (p. 69) on issues which society would prefer remain unvoiced and unquestioned. The *Radio* poems, with delightfully understated wit and humour, reflect the importance of the poet's relationship with language, communicating the understanding that in the realm of the poetic, as in the psychoanalytic, precision of language enables the articulation of something not heard before, that which normally resides outside of language, within the individual or societal unconscious or soul.

A sizable number of the poems in this collection is gathered under the theme of Spain. Michael's love of and connection with Spain, particularly with the region of Andalusia, form the basis of works detailing journeys and experiences at once physical, cultural, historical, emotional and spiritual. The various layerings in the poems describe a pilgrimage to territories of healing and belonging. The desire to become 'A courageous son of Spain' expressed in 'La Dama de Noche' (p. 43) evokes the spirit and work of Federico García Lorca, poet, playwright and son of Spain, whose work was inspired in large part by his native Andalusia. In their raw, sensuous descriptions of the landscape, history and culture of Andalusia as a realm which foregrounds aspects of life as a 'dance with God a dance with Death' (p. 50), Michael's poems both express and embody *duende*. Described by Lorca as 'the hidden spirit of our Spain of sorrows' which stretches across all barriers to reach the heart and the imagination, *duende* is the spirit possessing both art and artist, an essential element of authentic artistic production and performance, particularly within the indigenous Andalusian traditions of the bullfight and of flamenco music and dance. Those traditions' visceral expressivity, infused with *duende*, embody a proud and courageous affirmation of life in their confrontation with death, flamboyant and joyous in their expression of a spirit that death cannot silence. They have their exact poetic counterpart here in this collection. Those of us fortunate to have heard Michael use his voice to perform his poems have understood clearly the full meaning of Lorca's *duende*, and appreciate the bravura of *duende*'s artistic daring and grace when delivered by a master poet with an Irish accent.

While much of the work in this collection reflects the influences of Spain, it is important to underline that the poems remain grounded within an Irish literary tradition. In their expression of difficult truths often ignored or denied by contemporary societies, for example the pointlessness of life ('The Poppy'), or life's terror ('Season's Change') and ambivalence ('Auburn'), the poems gather together traditional strands common to both countries. The concept of *duende* is echoed in Ireland's *sean-nós* song and dance tradition, where life, love and death form a thematic unity and where, as *sean-nós* singer and scholar Lillis Ó Laoire describes, a concept similar to that of the Andalusian *duende* abides. The quality of *dúil* (desire) infuses and emanates from the *sean-nós* singer, undergirding a song performance permeated by *brí* (life force, meaning) and *misneach* (courage), both essential qualities of authentic or 'right' (*ceart*) performance which serves as a community celebration of life, often in defiance and subversion of societal restrictions. In both the Spanish and Irish traditions as articulated in Michael's work, the dance with death is what imbues life with much of its passion and meaning. While the concepts reflected in these traditions are not easily translated into English, Michael has succeeded in creating that 'new word yet to be spoken on earth' (p. 42). The meanings of those traditions are not readily accessible within modern/post-modern cultures intent on denying all that is associated with death, yet Michael captures the complex truth: 'So changed from having lost/ Aware of limits lacking that much more/ I embrace the cost of a new life/ A second time around' (p. 27). With a deep understanding of the significance of such cultural elements, Michael's work leads a dance with language and with the poetic form that renders visible, audible and vital that which lives at the edges of language and of contemporary Western culture.

If that which is best in the poetic imagination is bound to express a vision that extols a freedom both personal and human, the *Sexuality* poems within this volume speak of and to the horror and 'grotesquery' (p. 63) of the historical and contemporary treatment of homosexuality by various regimes of power and authority, illustrating the diminishment of all sexuality inherent in such positions. 'The People of the Book', establishing a dialogue between the voices of condemnation and the condemned, makes a powerful claim for the homosexual 'dialect of sexuality' to be given place as part of the shared language both of humanity and of spirituality. The *Sexuality* poems and the *Love* poems forge a theology of belonging and inclusion, built on love and compassion and manifested in the ordinary life – between partners and lovers, between parents and children – sacred in all its humanity. The voice that reaches out in understanding and generosity in 'To Those Who Have Given Up On Love' turns to celebration in 'Epithalmion: A Poem for Terry', from which the collection takes its name. Written as a gift to Michael's partner, Terry, on the occasion of their Civil Partnership Ceremony, the final poem in the collection gives voice to a simple, joyous celebration of love, which transcends the beloved, and celebrates the changes in Irish society that have enabled the public declaration and recognition of a dialect of love, hitherto condemned to a belowground silence and invisibility.

The Irish poet Eavan Boland has described poetry as 'a forceful engagement between a life and a language'. As a manifestation of such a rich, honest and deeply moving encounter, the work in Michael Murphy's wisdom collection of twenty-five poems unearths and creates exchanges and dialogues between personal and universal journeys, navigating and mapping the human geographies of the mind, body, heart and spirit. The poems stand as an eloquent expression of the sacrament of the fully inhabited life, revealing its homeland as a region without borders to which all belong and are invited to return. *The Republic of Love* exhorts us to accept that invitation; as we are reminded in 'Benedicite', 'Yes is a sacred word' (p. 102).

Dr Jeannine Woods
School of Languages, Literatures and Cultures,
National University of Ireland, Galway, 2013

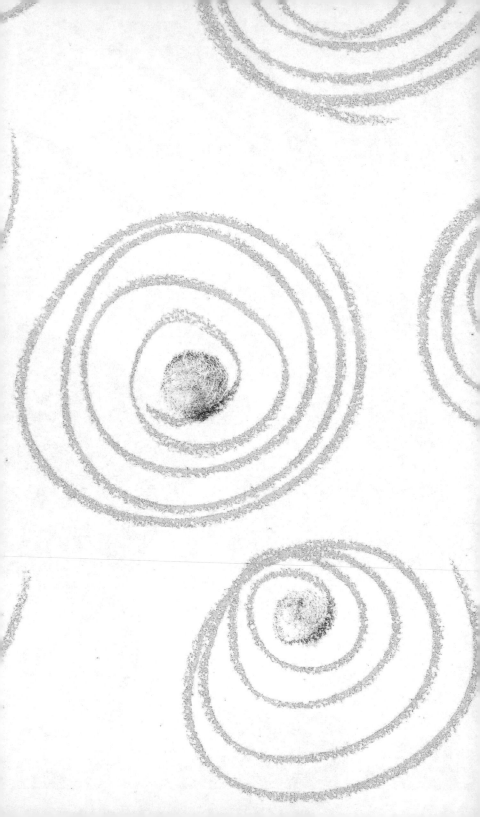

Flowers . . .

The Poppy

For the Athlone Community College Student
Award Winners 2010.

Because there is no point to anything anyway
It is necessary to be defiant and protesting
Like a single red poppy in a field of yellowing corn

And because I care so desperately that there is no point
I keenly feel the deadly sadness underlying it all

I know there is no voice that is like unto mine
There never was nor will there ever be again
For my time under the warmth of the sun which will set

And so there is no reason never to be
Outrageous or resplendent as a poppy
Bright-red
        erect
             and generously
Giving difference to the sameness of that field of corn
Shouting out that I was born for better or for worse
Waving my flag and making my colourful noise
And frightening away the darkness for as long as possible

To become the best poppy that ever there was
Is no mean ambition because it means
To take on the responsibility of caring for myself
And not to lean on or to take from others' kindnesses

And for today's eternity how glorious a thing it is
To be alive and laughing in the wind
Extravagantly scattering my seeds of happiness and hope
And being wild
               and flagrant
                  and dancing
Like a single red poppy in a whole field of yellowing corn

The Daffodil

For all those who have been touched by cancer.

I desire to be free as the daffodil
For daffodils dance in the wind and the rain
Like children at play laughing and waving
Celebrating in the green spring

Those brilliant yellow Lent lilies
Are risen from the dead after suffering underground
And offer the promise of a resurrection
Nodding their assent to the dream of the impossible

Their glance is more tenuous from having survived the
    past
Fearless of tomorrow they live only for today
And give prodigally blooming in profusion
Delighting the soul with yellow brightness
Inviting me courageously onwards towards the summer
Illuminating steps with lighted lanterns

So changed from having lost
Aware of limits lacking that much more
I embrace the cost of a new life
A second time around

Another chance to flame with love
The last dance better than before
I have endured like the daffodil
I too am above ground
And mostly I am childishly grateful

The Sunflower

The sunflower stares at the sun
It is held in a mutual gaze like a baby
Cradled in the bower of an arm
I place you at the centre of my life
To comfort you whenever you need me
I vow to keep you free from harm
Eternally

Underneath a cloudless sky
The summer heat lies heavy
On the fields of yellow sunflowers
That surround my whitewashed house in Spain
Protecting it like an army of smiling soldiers

From the brow of a hill thrust up into the blue
I survey the open faces of the troops
Marshalled in peaceful rows like Roman
     legionaries
Worshipping Mithras the god of searing light
Long ago
          In timeless Iberia

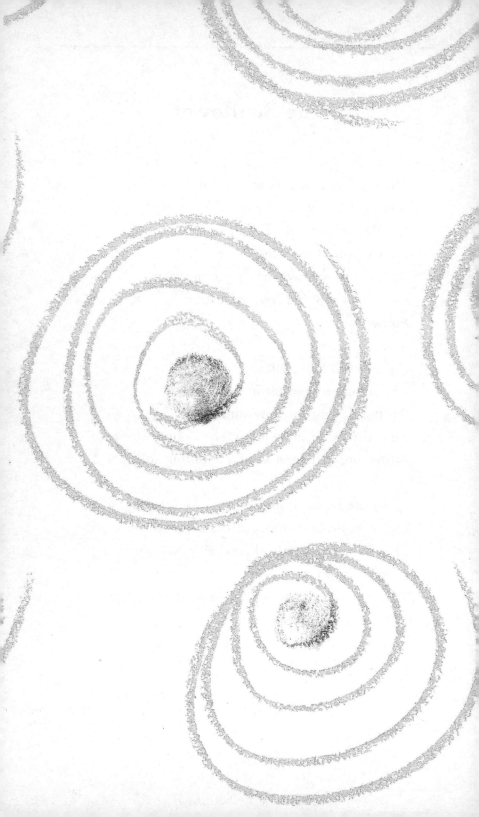

Spain . . .

Spain

The flaring light of Spain
Powders the air
With a dusting of white gold
Accumulating on the horizon
Leaching blue from the sky
A layering centuries old

The heightened light of Spain
Brimmed at my eyes
Like golden olive oil
And overflowed into my soul
Dripping unceasingly

The Pilgrim

It may be Guidera
That forebear of my great-grandmother
Set sail aboard a galleon
From Galicia

My father's sister Aunt Isabella remembered visiting
Two Guidera women
In the twenties
In Borris-in-Ossory
And my father always said his father
Had a sallow complexion like a Spaniard
We have the photograph to prove it
A Laois *campesino*
Rich with Guidera blood

Tradition in the family says Guidera was a guide
Who survived the Spanish Armada
Like St James *Matamoros*
Cast ashore and cut adrift
What did he feel
When first he saw the coast of Ireland?
To misapprehend the green like Galicia under the
    sun

For what was cold and unwelcoming as winter
What sort of map did Guidera have
That he could negotiate a shipwreck
In of all places Borris-in-Ossory?

Was he inured to harshness?
Did he experience tenderness
Charging the loins fuelling Irish lust
Some seventeen-year-old
With sallow skin and agile body
Exotic as Spanish olive oil?

Did they share a faith in common – this is my
    body –
Was their pleasure all the sweeter for Catholic
    guilt?
He traded her a name against another son for
    Spain
His children exiles in their own land
But she gave him place

Nevertheless the mystery remains:
What compass guided Guidera
And did he return to Spain
To reclaim his heritage?

Or did his son become the pilgrim?
Or was I the one to undertake
The Camino de Santiago
And bring his relics home?

Nöeleen

What do you do
When a woman gives you the gift of herself?
How do you repay that?

When she enfolds your hand in hers
And looks through your eyes
In an instant entrusting herself to what she sees there
What can you say in return?

I know a woman in Spain
Born at the time of the Christ child
Who takes the weft of God
And tries unendingly
To weave the threads of man through it
So that now you are always at the centre
And never at life's edge

How do I make amends
Or do I do you a disservice
By not responding in a new way?
Do you see the little boy
And know the meaning of the joy
That each new day's dawning brings for him?

You cut him free from the prism of ice that skews
    his light
By calling up the man
'Relax – it'll be all right – you're at your granny's'

Now that I am here in focus
What do you want of me?

Nothing
Utter indifference
I be me in my way
You be you in yours
And from the tension of the opposites
We create together the Godhead
A new word yet to be spoken on earth
So that I can continue
To weave my thread through
Haven't you heard it yet?

I need you for this
That is why I never stand in any man's light
She gently polished my forehead with a kiss
'Shine' she whispered
'Shine' I said
And I switched on
The universe

La Dama De Noche

La Dama de Noche her perfume
Visited me in my room
She suffused me with scent
Tried to seduce me with blandishments
'You know' she said 'that Spain has set a table
Just for you under the sun'
It was natural not to yield, to question 'Why?
  Why me?'
While this simple extravagance of La Dama's gift
  required the response 'Why not?'

She was insistent that place-setting was mine
'It's in your name' she said 'If you don't fill it, then
  who will?'
The initial choice it seems was made by Spain
In the ninth month of ninety-nine I was born a child
  of light
Dare I disturb the universe and make that choice my
  own?
If I refuse it will be as if I never had been
Withering without taking root
If I assent then all I had been I will lose

I desire to take my place
To flower in daylight
Scenting the air with my presence
I desire to espouse La Dama de Noche
And become a powerful man in the bounteous
    banquet of life
Under the nurturing sun of Spain
So that I in my turn can give light
And become in my turn
A courageous son
Of Spain

Season's Change

Autumn arrived early this morning
So unexpectedly in Elviria

I surfaced from a dreamless sleep shrouded in sweat
And blundered to the bathroom to piss and wet the
　floor tiles

The leaves of the *palmeras* barked in the sudden
　levanter
Souls that got lost in their solitude out past Tarifa
Saw me inside and rattled their bones
Begging for the love of Allah
I had to close the window on their terror

When I awoke the whole area was being painted
With wraiths of cold mist which dimmed the lustre
Savaging the sunlight writing shape-shifting
　cuneiform
Characters telling me that autumn had arrived

In a shiver of circling black and white storks
Hundreds of them turning around overhead
Streaming south in the thermals
Drawing ghosts in their wake

I thought or heard or read a despairing scream in
    autumn's echo
Just before the fog burnt up the tale of the damned
In the blazing searing heat of the Costa del Sol
    summer

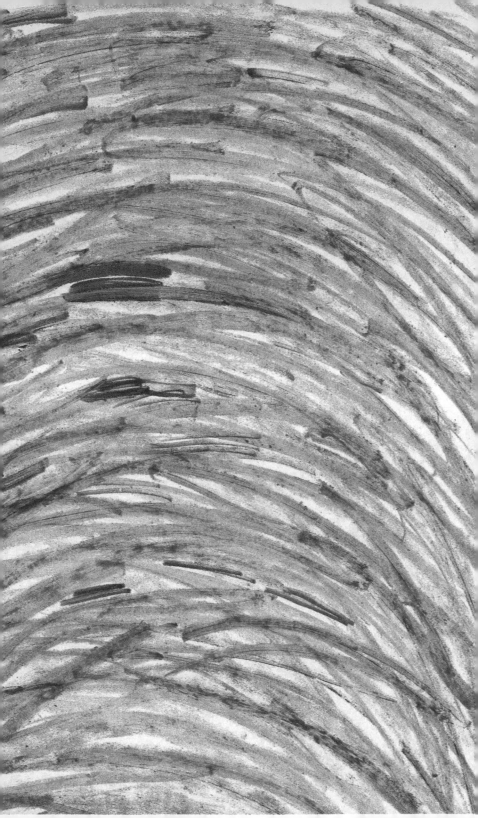

Christmas

We lost Christmas on the Costa del Sol
The windy coast it was closed 'No peoples . . . '
An English couple hanging on to Santa hats
And bottle trophies from a garage supermarket
Supported one another

At lunch alone we looked
And silently fleeing Bing Crosby's 'White Christmas'
Stammering tips in the pizzeria in Elviria
Escaped to where?
¡Feliz navidad!

La Concha

Red is the colour of Marbella's mountain
Scrawled in God's fresh blood beneath the blue-veined
   sky
An outing covenant danced in black
With clacking heels across this tract of plain
The flourish of a final turn reveals
A red-emblazoned serpent shimmering

Red is the colour of God's signature
Slumbering under a clear blue sky
A red mountain mantra inscribed across
The talisman of a reflecting frieze
Evoking the latent voice of God
A ruby-red rioja from the juice of blackened grapes

Red is the *muleta* trailed by God across the sand
A red flamenco frock swirling like the wild levanter
Plunging to the hilt to the heart the sword
A roaring gush of vivid red unfurling
Cruel as the reddest sun that rises suddenly
Searing those stamping footsteps into the black bull's
   skin

Red is the colour of Marbella's mountain
Kohled black eyes shaded behind mantilla grilles
The far-off gaze of God is straight and proud unwavering
A red paper flower flies to earth from out of this dancer's
hair
And is kicked to the side in a flounce of strutting skirts
It creates the red arena for the inevitable ending
Of a final dance with God a dance with Death

Tarifa

The wind always blows on the beach at Tarifa
Sweeping along the sand folding and unfolding
Whipping up the grains into the sizzling air
And tossing them about like the kite-flyer angels
With colourful wings skimming across the breaking
   waves
Fallen angels sand-blasted black against the scorching
   sun
Polished by unbearable light stepping out of the sea
In a glittering cloud of glory embodying
The same unchanging message for mankind
The wind always blows on the beach at Tarifa

God walks in the wind on that beach at Tarifa
He presses his lips to the shore in a kiss
And leaves his spittal frothing on the sand
He whistles through the pines by the drifting dunes
He writes his name writhing like a snake
And when he turns the locals say that meat goes bad
His gaze is ferocious screaming out of the storm
Burning my soul with his psychotic certainties
The wind always blows on the beach at Tarifa

I contended with my God on that beach at Tarifa
We leaped together into the turbulent air
Holding hands like lovers ascending
Wheeling around exulting up into the blue
I held his implacable gaze against the sun
And I reproached him for life having happened to me
He plundered the complaint from my mouth with the
    wind
But I listened to my lamentation moaning desolately in
    the trees
As we soared towards an acceptance of what is
And I refused it as not being good enough
I withheld compliance from the inevitable ending
Of just another grain of sand being scattered by the
    breeze
For the wind always blows on the beach at Tarifa

I dared to dream I chose to shine
Like the evanescent morning star
Or to behave like the brightest shooting star falling from
    heaven
I am my own man I said and thought of Lucifer and
    Luther
I courageously claimed freedom for even the shortest
    arc of time
Knowing that my glorious revolt precedes a restoration
For the wind always blows on that beach at Tarifa

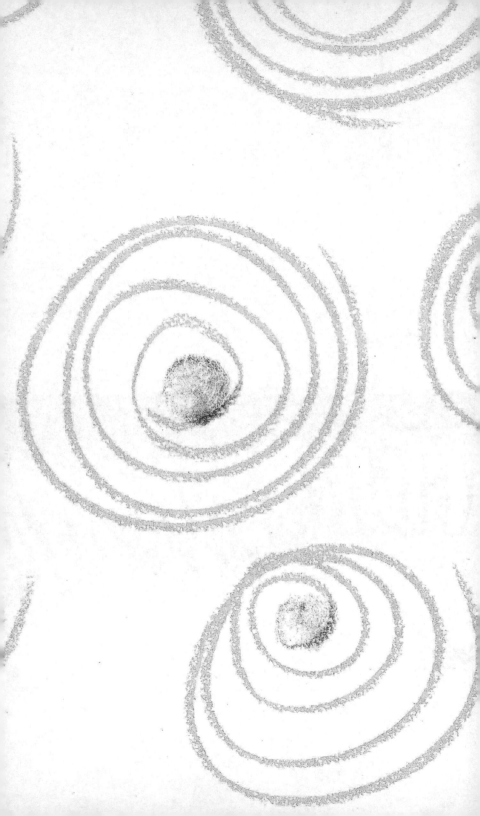

Sexuality . . .

An Ode to Those Labelled
'Intrinsically Disordered'

We remember the terror of the men and of the women
Who are still denounced
Once they were burned at the stake
Their lives extinguished at Buchenwald
Who are still in prison

To have a legal way of being
                              powerless
Because they happen to be homosexual

I owe them so much honour

The People of the Book

The People of the Book
Condemn me for being
A person who loves
Those of my own sex

The Christians the Muslims
And even the Jews
(Who attest to the lack of redemption)
Believe that God says
For me to be loving
I'd have to be living in sin

The Nazis decided I'm *'unter-mensch'*
A subhuman person
To be burned in the ovens at Buchenwald
The German Pope
Following on in that tradition
Decreed that as a human being
I'm 'intrinsically disordered . . .
With a tendency towards evil'
A ranking so far beneath
That of the heterosexual elect

I'm destined to be burned in the fires of hell
For all eternity

The People of the Book
See nothing wrong with that prejudice
They consider themselves nice people
'If it were up to them . . . ' But it's not
God is the despot here

The People of the Book believe
I have a dialect of sexuality
Which must be suppressed
For the sake of the family
Or because the 'grotesquery' of gay marriage
Poses 'the biggest threat to our civilisation'
Bigger even than global warming
(I recall from those harrowing documentaries on
    television
The same threat was once laid at the door of the Jews)
Do the People of the Book hope that the millions of us
Will be obliterated off the face of the earth?
Or should we voluntarily submit ourselves to castration
    by dogma
For differing sexually from the majority?

The People of the Book
Ignore the advances in human psychology
Which say that my dialect of sex
Is a normal outcome of the Oedipus complex
They say they take their instruction
From Moses and Jesus and Muhammad
Whom they preach with all the fanatical certainty
Of the ignorant and insecure

The People of the Book suggest
That I should press my sexuality
Between the leaves of the good book
So that it can wither away like a desiccated flower
For according to them my 'out' sexuality
Is not orthodox not sanctioned
By people who monopolise the deity

The tragedy for me
Is that the People of the Book
Would exclude me from a sense of the sacred
Which I find in the wonder of love
And in the various expressions of human nature

I can hear God speak through the human voice
That tells me I'm all right despite my differences

That encourages me to continue on when times get
    tough
Helping me to hope for better
That is humble enough to walk beside me on the road
On every journey of my life
That makes a commitment to a fellow human being
Reaching out to lift the heavy burden off my
    shoulders
That trusts me unconditionally with the courage
To live out my truth in spite of doubt
Responsible only to the best that I can be
Flowering in my own way and at my own pace
Without feeling the need to berate me as the
    scapegoat
The outsider the stranger
The prodigal son the neighbour

That can always say to me the Jew
Me the Christian me the Muslim
Me the son of God
'I believe in you
Because I love you'

And also (a dialect the People of the Book conveniently
    forget)
'Because you are mine' says the Lord

Emotions . . .

A Dignified Silence

Against a three-year-old child
Being beaten to within an inch of his life
We have maintained a dignified silence

Against a seven-year-old child
Being sexually molested by several men
We have maintained a dignified silence

Against a teenager
Coping with the strain of an alcoholic father
We have maintained a dignified silence

Against a gay twenty-year-old
Daring to come out to an unaccepting world
We have maintained a dignified silence

Against my brother wasting away from cancer
Living out of love as long as possible
We have maintained a dignified silence

Against myself attacked by prostate cancer
Without continence still impotent
We have maintained a dignified silence

And for you my brother we would have wished the same
Not to speak about the horror nor to have had your say
But to take your stand with us in maintaining to the last
A dignified silence

On Contemplation

Here in this *terra incognita*
I vanquish with Apollo what is
Familiar to me from before:
The insular, ghostly, grey sea-mist.

In a ritual morning battle
The deadening gloom is put to flight,
And the blinding light shines in triumph
All the day long, from skies the colour
Of lapis lazuli.

            I hear the
Clicking afternoon heat lie heavy
As a bed-sheet, cast aside from the
Boiling vastness of this rumpled,
Lurid land. I cry out at the sight
Of lemons fallen from trees. I turn
Towards the sweetly fragrant jasmine
Wafting in the breeze. I take delight
In rough hewn walls, imprinting whitewash
On my hands, these Cubist surrounds of
Andalus *pueblos*.

               In further
Exploring the newness, I taste the
Golden fruit of the sun: pressed oil
From olives locally grown.

                         I am
Describing here contemplation, a
Mode of being where my voice soars
Across the face of heaven with the
Sun. From this vantage point, I can
Look back at those I left behind, and
Measure how far I have come, recall
All the pioneering lands through which
I passed to reach here

                    and find treasure.

Fear

I feel afraid all the time
Fear is my default setting
I grin and greet people
Inside I feel terrified

At the end of a pier in the dark
I fold up my clothes in a bundle
I leave my car keys in my shoes
And slip silently over the edge
Drowning in a winter sea

What toppled the terror over?
Too weighty suddenly
A flight into the lapping blackness
So that I continue to fall forever
Frozen with fear

Don't hand on the shock to others
'If only we had known
We would have done something . . . '
I have always known
There was nothing
I could have done differently

I have excavated the truth
Excoriated it with words
So that it was stripped bare
To the bone

The skeletal face of a drowning man
The rigid open mouth
No resources left
No protective skin
The unavailing barrier of a hollow grin

Too much suffocating truth

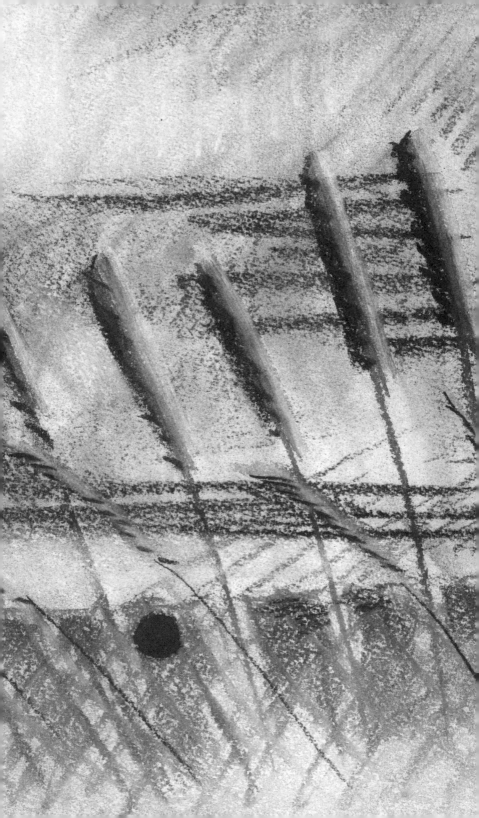

Radio . . .

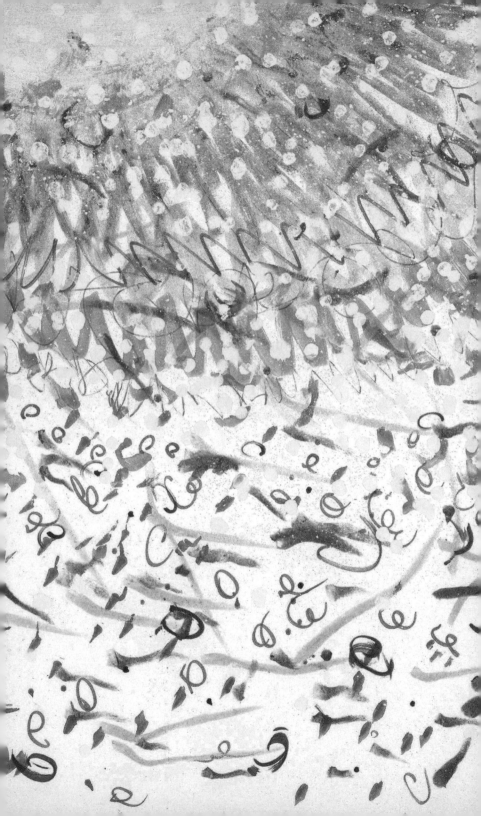

Radio Four

I want to live in Radio Four
Where the accents are creamily redolent
Of Cotswold stone
                where I overheard the writer
Joanna Trollope say 'I once
Had a friend who revived a panicked sheep
With an entire bottle of rescue remedy'
Guests paint a picture with proper words
Pronounced with care
                I long to live there

Here is the News

The announcer came on at six o'clock in the morning
She wished us all a 'Happy Gnu Year!'
And said 'Over now to Michael Murphy in the Gnu's
    room . . . '

For a second I was struck dumb
Affronted
Then I recovered myself

A gnu is an antelope
Which inhabits the savannahs of Africa
I've seen it on television
It has an ox-like head and a long tufted tail

I knew that a gnu was a mythical beast as well
Believed to live along the banks of the River
    Euphrates
But 'Happy Gnu Year' made no sense to me

'Over now to Michael Murphy in the Gnu's room'
Sounded denigrating perhaps a comment
On the supposed wildebeest habits of my newsroom
    colleagues

I could never begin a bulletin with 'Here is the gnus'
Because the sentence is grammatically incorrect
It should read 'Here are the gnus' by way of introducing
The herd of springbok and impala
The blackbuck and the dikdik
That would suddenly proliferate inexplicably in a news
    script

In my forty years as a broadcaster
I've never had to do that: 'Here is the news' yes
'Here are the gnus' no
So when I hear the announcer go
'Happy Gnu Year' I want to become a hunter like Ernest
    Hemingway
And yes I want to kill but not a helpless animal
Rather somebody who should have known better
Than to take me unawares and profane my writer's ear
    at six o'clock in the morning

I question whether a radio station
Grounded as it is in the spoken word
Can be taken seriously
If it doesn't make an effort to sound intelligent

We are all bound to find ourselves in language
A common property that we turn into a personal tool to
    communicate
What impression did our Taoiseach make
On foreign heads of state
When he mangled his syntax?
Was he saved by the skills of the translator?
How can today's poets write poetry? It's not possible
If they don't know that constable rhymes with cup
Or that precedent turns into a cupboard and becomes
    un-*press*-edented when they put an 'un' in front of it.

A writer or speaker implies
What a reader or hearer infers
So somebody talking about an antelope at six o'clock in
    the morning
Leads me to reason since I am enfolded into that broadcast
That I'm being wished a happy year as a bovid or as a
    mammal

But if a presentation announcer was parading
Her basic ignorance of English speech
By invoking a procession of graceful gazelle
When her intention was merely to send out a greeting
And simply to wish us well in the coming year
What hope is there of legal safety from uncaring savages

Even if we seek justice in a thicket of linguistic
    difference and truth?

What hope is there of relating openly to my fellow-man
    my brother
And being nourished by his care and by his love
If one word can sound and mean the same as any Annie
    other udder?

Eau De

I closed the microphone
And slowly released with relief
A pent-up plosive reverberating very early morning fart
Into the close confines
Of the tiny news heads' studio

The enveloping odour was of old wet dog
With intimate notes of decaying dead rat
Trapped beneath the floorboards
So poisonously acrid
'It'd take the brand off a sack' as my late father used to say
Way beyond any ineffectual dispersal
Through waving a news script at the fumes
From behind the chair

When I opened the microphone again
The door burst open
And in walked Pauric Lodge
To read the sports news

The revised Christmas schedule contains
Many such rich surprises

I hadn't the heart to chide him
For the overpowering stench
Of his expensive eau de toilette
Which filled the studio with
A very welcome Christmas gift

We sat opposite each other
In a warm but impregnable silence
Preparing our scripts for the broadcast
Each of us almost afraid to breathe

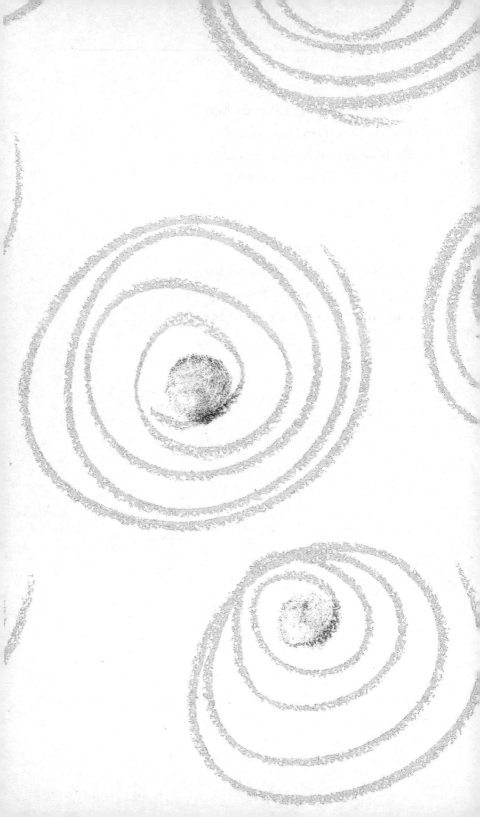

Love . . .

To Those Who Have
Given Up On Love

To those who have given up on love
I reach out my hand
Shivering at the depth of your personal despair
I shut my mouth on intrusive questions
Is it because you feel unworthy
Or has life unfairly passed you by

Here is a hand you can hold on to
For a while
For whatever reason
If that is what you want
Although I know it's not
Enough
Until you find your footing once again
And you will
Inevitably
Fall
And recover slower
And with less resilience
As you grow
Older

Put your hand in mine
And let the warmth of my embrace
Begin to thaw the neglect that you have lived with
Withering away from winter's harsh unfeeling winds
Smiling mysteriously to conceal a broken heart
Your embarrassing pain
Too apparent to everyone
As out of place here
As the suppurating wound of your grief

I can see that others have hurt you
You've suffered from the cruelty of carelessness
From the thoughtless exuberance of youth
From the smugness of coupledom

A reluctant invitation to attend at their table
Generously delighting
In someone else's happiness
Then left brusquely on your own
To take a taxi home
At the end of the occasion
Resuming your life
As a single oddity

Will you not reach out to touch my hand
It's the hand of a baby
So that I can grasp at even your littlest finger

Inviting you to fan the spark of love to flame
I need to take delight
In the flicker of your smile
To be happily confirmed
In the mirror of your eyes
Can't you see that I have just begun
On the road you have travelled
That today I need to hold on to you as guide
Will you be that other for me now
Until I find my feet
And grow tall as a sunflower
Under love's beaming smile

I need to believe in life
I need to believe in love
To experience even once in my lifetime an us
Do you remember when there was an us
Do you remember what the softest kiss felt like
Brushed with loving lips up over your tingling skin
Or the sweet smell of someone's body lying asleep
    beside you
Or the supportive touch of their hand as they held onto
    your heart
And broke it open before your startled eyes
Like a luscious fig

And did both of you taste of it then
When love was new
In spring

Recall it to your mind
And tell me what it means to you
What love has meant across your lifetime
Tell me
Was the pleasure worth it
Would you do it all again
Despite the pain
Will you tell me the truth
As much as I can bear
Of love and intimacy
And trust and sex
Tell me of the person that you loved
And who loved you
Once upon a time
When it was ever summer

To those of us who have given up on love
Unlock your secrets from the deep
Set them free to walk upon this earth
Like the tallest guardian angels
Flaming with the light of love
So that they can pierce your flesh once again with
    passion's sword

I know these prisoners are constrained within your
   heart
I know you are the poorer for living a half-life
The best of you smothered
Underneath the ashes of your loving achievement
Remember it now
And share it aloud
With those who have given up on love
Wear the clothes of the love story of your life
And look resplendent
Shining proud for me

I appeal to those who have given up on love
Please don't give up on us
It is never too late to continue to love
So please don't give up on you
And please don't you give up on me

Auburn – For Mary

*Auburn is the name of a Georgian house in Malahide,
County Dublin, the home of my friend Mary. This poem
refers to Ferdia, who suffered from motor neurone disease,
and who has sadly passed away.*

Faced with my helplessness
Not knowing how to help
I placed my hand under his elbow
And welcomed Ferdia home

We were married once
We have three children together
We found ourselves at a place
Where he didn't want to be

It hurts too much to be intimate
Now that this has happened again
I have some idea what it means
To have hope stolen
To fear for the future
So I touch him lightly on the elbow
Knowing there's no cure

We communicate through writing
As though he were still absent
He types a reply on his laptop
Attempting to correct the predictor
And I get called away

The tragedy of losing a voice
Enduring the pain, surviving
Alone with no redemption
Too much for anyone to bear

So I place my hand under his elbow
Helping Ferdia home

Celibate Men in Dresses

Celibate men in dresses
Have captured God
Like an exotic wild animal
They try to keep him caged
Behind the tall narrow walls of their tradition
They scarcely give God room to breathe in the darkness

For centuries celibate men in dresses
Have excluded the feminine
Yet the Holy Spirit is feminine
And always partakes in the joy of the trinity
The assumption of a real woman into heaven
Makes the balance two male plus two female
Four is God's whole number

Celibate men in dresses
Exist without irony
In a world of feudal overlords
And absolute monarchs
They expect to command our attention
While we get on with our lives
Too kind to tell them the truth
Too busy to be bothered

Oblivious that celibate men in dresses
Have been refused their intrusion
Into heterosexual relationships
Diverting attention instead
Onto their latest out group
Today they mount an unrelenting inquisition
Against gay people

The commandant at Buchenwald
Where homosexuals were persecuted to death
Also had a private zoo for exotic animals
God was at home there among his prisoners

No kissing of the ring
There is no sleight of hand that can cover over the
    crime
Of upholding an institution of mitred prelates
At the expense of innocent children abused

Celibate men in dresses
Have continually crucified God
Not only in the stranger
They have forbidden the second coming of his
    resurrection
In the magisterium of his chosen people
A designation withdrawn from Jerusalem
And now definitively lost to those in Rome

Because God cannot be contained
Whatever his sexuality

Celibate men in dresses
Are neither real men
Nor inferior substitutes for real women
Real men and women feel the breath of God's own
    spirit
On their naked skin as they make love
They set God free to play like the wind
And incarnate in their humanity
They grow up to be ordinary mothers and fathers
They are not infallible
They are never made into saints
But God entrusts his children to them
He shines out of the light in their eyes
He runs free in their fun and in their laughter
For love is where holiness is found

Young mothers and fathers are heroes of love
They sacrifice all for their little ones
Older men and women have proven their holiness
They give joyful service to others for the long haul
God is moving silently in the open hearts of his chosen
    people

He can be glimpsed in the warmth of their
    loving relationships

Weighed down like a millstone
With embroidered brocade and the finest lace
Celibate men wear dresses
Of the sheerest irrelevance
Because God has escaped their constraints
Untamed and unprotected
Always wild forever free
And celibate men in dresses
Guard cages that are empty
Nothing left to say
Because everything is frozen

In the end
There was no word

Gloria In Excelsis

Like a wise man following a star
I bring my gifts on Christmas Day
To the baby in the crib
I leave behind anxiety
Protect the cradled child from life's pessimism
If I no longer believe in a redeemer divine

Surrounded by the smell of pine and evergreens
I light a silent candle for the dead
Remembering the candle in the window
And the long-ago welcome home on Christmas Eve

The children's story of no room at the inn
And the superstition of my grown-up sensibilities
Equally excluded from the humble scene within
I bring imaginative possibilities to the framing
    from without
Of a young mother with her newborn baby
A practical commitment to the business of the present
A careful reverence for life continuing on
Discerning mystery amidst the ordinary straw

This Christmas Day has been born in Bethlehem
A saviour
I am my own redeemer

I whisper a prayer and muster help with hope
I say to the midwinter gloom of an empty universe
I am alive thank God
For those with whom I live and love
I can try to make things better
And bring glory to the highest heavens
Gloria in excelsis

Benedicite

for Jeanne and Mark

*Benedicite means a blessing — literally, to say well.
This poem was read at their wedding in University
Church, St Stephen's Green, Dublin, on
22 December 2012.*

'Yes' is a courageous commitment
As delicate as the air that it displaces
To be received with reverence
And venerated for its holiness

'Yes' is an assent to life
An annunciation heard
Nine months before the nativity
A foundation stone on which
To build a home within
'Yes' is a sacred word

She shyly proffered us the ring
A glittering diamond crystal
That seemed to be floating on air
'We got engaged this Christmas Eve' she said

They both were beaming happily
Inviting praise and recognition
Commending themselves to each other
And to us for their achievement

'I had a dream that I was choosing children's names'
   he said
'Middle-class names of saints like Paul and Mark
She was sure of the ring in the window
So I asked her marry me'
She said 'Not like this not now outside a jeweller's
   shop'
And then she said 'Why not . . . ?'

Such is the logic of how lives intertwine
The pattern of how decisions are arrived at
Commitments that are timed to coincide irregularly
Cut like the facets of a diamond ring
Facing away from each other

They were walking back arm in arm
To their car in the Phoenix Park
When a stranger had called after them
'You look well together'
Setting them up to suit each other
For a whole lifetime of continuous hope

'Yes' a feather-light kiss to the forehead
'Yes' a whispered grace
'Yes' the tenderest of looks
And a determined proclamation
'Yes' is the bravest undertaking
Of all the continuous covenants

For unto us is born from heaven above
On every Christmas morning of our lives
Love the divine redeemer
Benedicite
Say 'yes'

Epithalamion: A Poem for Terry

*An epithalamion is a poem or song traditionally
composed to celebrate a wedding. It was first recited on
the occasion of our Civil Partnership Ceremony,
14 June 2011.*

When I grow old and have no voice
No children there to care or to remember me
I shall always know
That there was once a midsummer's day in Dublin
When I was loved

Then I shall smile in the dreamtime
Hearing once more
The dawn chorus announced with trumpet blasts
And see the vivid roses burst into bloom
And twine around the morning of that glorious day in
    June
When I was finally allowed
To be loved

I shall laugh inside through Stephen's Green
And leave my dancing footprints in the dew

So you can follow me
And take your place
By my side
On a day which was prepared
Since the beginning of the world
For you are my world
And I have always loved you

Whenever I would look into your questioning eyes
    of blue
To find myself reflected in your goodness
I could never feel afraid of others' judgement
Or their shame at these extolling words
As true as you have proved to be
For an everyday eternity
Of table fellowship and fun

The sun swept to attention and saluted us at noon
We did not stand in one another's shadow
When we vowed either to each
Three times before our family of like-minded friends
Who have supported us for better or for worse

The words were tolling in the golden air
They bathed us in light so that we shone

I shall honour you with my esteem
   because of your integrity
I promise to support and bear the weight
Of your open unprotected soul
I promised too to love you, as if ever I had stopped
And needed to commence what is continuous
And round as the ring you gave to me
Blessed with your affection

On that laughing summer's day
The wind was cheering and the leaves on the trees
   were waving
As we processed towards our future through O'Connell
   Street
Side by side we laid our bouquet of roses out at the
   GPO
Acknowledged those who gave their lives so we could
   be cherished equally
Proclaimed ourselves free
                and free to become
Better together than either of us could choose to
   achieve on our own
And we withdrew relevance from those who
   disapproved
Of our new and mutual republic of love

There is nothing I regret more than my compliance
That I was not in my life more undignified and
    reckless and awkward
Like you a fearless fighter joyfully at home in foreign
    lands
An encourager of dreams an explorer of the soul's
    secrets
And warm and tender as the pleasure of our private
    trysts

Whenever we shall be no more and nobody
`   remembers us
These words of mine shall inherit the earth
They will echo in the heart of every season
That there was once a midsummer's day in Dublin
When I was loved
                        and they will sing out loud
    my song
Repeat publicly the poem I have told about you
And the treasure you endowed me with
The inestimable adventure of a meaningful life

This simple shining truth shall belong to you
    immortally

That once upon a time
                    on a Dublin midsummer's
     day at noon
I always loved you

Then you will be moving in the wind and in the
    trees
And especially when the roses are in bloom
You will gladden with a smile or with a glance
When people feel your presence in the wonder
    of beautiful words
Lingering in a room like your fragrance
The blown petals falling to earth like prayers
Whispering over and over that I have always
    loved you
That I have loved you, too

www.michaelmurphyauthor.com

If you've enjoyed reading this poetry book, then please tell others about it, and recommend *The Republic of Love* to your friends.

And if you'd like to let me know how my poems have affected you, you can email me at the following address: info@michaelmurphyauthor.com. I'd welcome receiving your comments and insights. And while protecting your identity, I'd also be happy to put your response on my website: www.michaelmurphyauthor.com.

For your added enjoyment, the website gives background information on *The Republic of Love*. It also gives information about the various book-signings and readings around the country, where I look forward to having an opportunity to meet you. You'll find the latest news there about how *The Republic of Love* has been received by the professional critics. There's also a section on this website dealing with my first book, *At Five in the Afternoon – My Battle With Male Cancer*, and its sequel, *The House of Pure Being*.

Finally, I want to thank you for taking the time to read my poems. I hope you felt it was a rewarding experience.

Go dté tu slán!